Hiking with Dogs

*Becoming a wilderness-wise
dog owner*

Linda B. Mullally

FALCON®

HELENA, MONTANA

AFALCONGUIDE®

Falcon® is continually expanding its list of recreational guidebooks. All books include detailed descriptions, accurate maps, and all the information necessary for enjoyable trips. You can order extra copies of this book and get information and prices for other Falcon® guidebooks by writing Falcon, P.O. Box 1718, Helena, MT 59624 or calling toll-free 1-800-582-2665. Please ask for a free copy of our current catalog. Visit our website at www.FalconOutdoors.com or contact us by e-mail at falcon@falcon.com.

Illustrations by Todd Telander

Library of Congress Cataloging-in-Publication Data

Mullally, Linda B.
  Hiking with dogs : becoming a wilderness-wise dog owner / Linda B.
Mullally ; [illustrations by Todd Telander].
    p. cm.
  Includes bibliographical references.
  ISBN 1-56044-817-2 (pbk.)
  1. Hiking with dogs. I. Title.
SF427.455.M85 1999
796.51—dc21   99-24775
                                                                         CIP

CAUTION

Outdoor recreation can be dangerous. Everyone who goes into the wilderness or backcountry assumes some risk and responsibility for his or her own actions and safety. The information contained in this book is a summary of the author's personal experiences, research, review of existing literature on dogs, and conversations with dog training experts. However, neither this book (nor any other book) can ensure your safety from the elements. Nor can this book (or any other book) replace sound judgment and good decision-making skills, which will greatly reduce the risks of going into the wilderness.

Learn as much as possible from this book and other sources of information, and prepare for the unexpected. Be safe and cautious. The reward will be a safer and more enjoyable experience.

Contents

Preface and Acknowledgments

My love of hiking with my dog began in childhood between the banks of the St. Maurice and St. Lawrence Rivers in Trois-Rivieres, Quebec. On weekends I would leave the house at dawn with my best friend, Sophie, a grey miniature poodle, and we would disappear for hours to explore the wooded shores of the St. Maurice River. Since then, I have hiked thousands of miles of trails around the globe. My peak experiences are encased in every nature walk and backpacking trip shared with my two dogs, Lobo and Shiloh, during the past eight years. I am forever indebted to them for enhancing my love affair with hiking and nature and for inspiring this book.

I also want to acknowledge the following people for their valuable contribution to this project: my husband, David (who never had a dog as a child), for opening his mind and heart to the adventure of loving and living with Lobo and Shiloh and for convincing me I had something important to share with other dog owners; George Bishop, DVM, for his sound professional advice and opinions; my brothers, Russell, Peter, and Dani, for their continual support of my passion for dogs and my compassion for the environment; my mom and dad (now deceased) for their understanding of my love of dogs and the outdoors; the team of workers and policymakers at dog-friendly Garland Ranch Regional Park in Carmel Valley, California, for providing Lobo, Shiloh, and hundreds of other dogs with almost 5,000 acres of hiking trails to safely romp and sniff during their rambunctious puppyhood and spirited adulthood; and Henri Boudreau, the English composition teacher who first put the pen in my hand and nurtured my love for the written word.

Thank you to fellow dog lovers and hikers: Phil Mallek, Molly Attell, Ronda Copeland, Tom Deyerle, and Gerry Van Hook for their input and enthusiastic participation.

A special thanks to park ranger Robert Chapin; Susie Bluford, dog trainer and breeder; Pat Tucker, wildlife biologist and cofounder of Wild Sentry, an environmental education organization; and Cindy Cather, dog groomer, for their time and expertise. I am grateful to all the National Park Service and USDA Forest Service personnel in Washington, D.C., who eagerly answered my questions and directed me through the maze of departments in my search for useful resources for dog owners.

Why Hike with Your Dog?

The difference between walking and hiking is not distance; rather it is the difference between a stroll in a city park versus an escape into the high Sierra. Urban pressures recede as you gorge on fresh air and scenic open space and delight in your dog's exuberance in the natural world.

Hiking also provides time for quality bonding between owner and dog. Dog owners with busy schedules find that hiking is a convenient opportunity to combine their own need and their dog's need for exercise and play in a safe, natural setting. Exercise from hiking can be excellent prevention for physical and behavioral disorders and in some cases helps reduce the symptoms of other ailments.

One in three dogs in America is overweight, which is usually a result of feeding too much (often the wrong foods) and moving too little. As in humans, obesity can trigger more serious health problems including heart attack, high blood pressure, diabetes, or even arthritis. To determine how fit your dog is, use this simple rule: You should be able to feel her ribs when you run your hands along her sides (*feel* them, not *see* them).

The stress on the joints from carrying the extra weight can also exacerbate preexisting conditions like hip dysplasia. The exercise from hiking can help keep your dog trimmer and strengthen muscles that support the hips.

Hiking also helps dogs that suffer from boredom, depressive lethargy, or other destructive behaviors. Regular exercise outdoors can help mellow out high-strung dogs and dogs prone to overt dominance and aggression.

Hiking is a natural and enjoyable way for people and dogs to stay fit. Running up a dirt trail, leaping over streams, climbing on boulders, negotiating fallen limbs in the forest, and paddling circles in a lake keep a dog's spirit soaring and her body agile, trim, and toned.

Hiking is a healthy, noncompetitive, and inexpensive form of recreation. As a dog owner, you have the opportunity to enhance the hiking experience with your live-in hiking companion. Your dog's innate curiosity, alertness, and intuitiveness can give you an added sense of appreciation and security.

HAPPY TRAILS!

Time and thought invested in preparing to hike with your dog will be rewarded with hours of safe, fun recreation on the trail.

2
Choosing a Dog for the Trail

Dogs have always been great companions. But certain physical and personality traits of certain breeds make some dogs better hiking companions than others.

HIKING POTENTIAL BY BREED

Although dogs should be evaluated on their individual merits, having an idea of what the dog (purebred or mixed breed) was originally bred to do helps you adjust your expectations about hiking potential. There are over 400 breeds of dogs recognized around the world, varying in size, appearance, and abilities. From the largest (Irish wolfhound) to the smallest (Chihuahua), all retain a somewhat instinctive link to their wild roots.

Primitive Dog Breeds

This small group of natural dogs is believed to have its origin with the Asian Wolf. Dogs with "primitive" stock are often defined by how minimally selective breeding has interfered with their natural legacy: Medium size and balanced proportions for enduring swiftness on the hunt, prick eared, pointed muzzles, short to medium length coats, alert and aloof.

Breed examples: basenji, pharaoh hound, Australian cattle dog. Dingoes and New Guinea singing dogs.

Positive hiking traits: good stamina, agile, alert.

Concerns: Slow maturing, requiring more intense bonding and more time to respond to obedience training; strong

St. Bernard   *Dachshund*

Irish Wolfhound

Chihuahua

hunting instincts that require patient, continuous reinforcement of impulse-control training or life at the end of a leash to prevent chasing wildlife.

Sight and Scent Hounds

Bred to detect and track prey by superior sight and scent. Sight Hounds are now being bred more for companionship than hunting.

Breed examples: greyhound, whippet, Afghan (sight hounds); bloodhound, basset hound, beagle (scent hounds).

Positive hiking traits: thrive on physical activity.

PHYSICAL TRAITS THAT GET IN THE WAY
• Thick or dark coats absorb more heat, causing your pet to overheat more easily.
• Thick coats become heavy when wet and can turn a tired dog into a drowning dog.
• Long coats act like Velcro around some grasses and burrs (consider a "trail trim").
• Hairless breeds are more susceptible to sunburn and cold (sunscreen and doggie sweaters are essential accessories).
• Short-legged dogs may have difficulty negotiating some trail conditions, which can slow your pace and affect the length of your hikes.
• Short-muzzled dogs (e.g., pugs, boxers) are more susceptible to overheating during exertion because their short sinus passages do not cool air as efficiently.

Concerns: Sight hounds instinctively want to chase small animals, including small dogs. Chasing all that moves is of particular concern with retired race dogs like greyhounds. The Afghan's coat is high maintenance, whereas the whippet's thin skin is vulnerable to scratches and gashes on the trail. Most hounds are a challenge to obedience train and the whiff of an interesting scent can send them off wandering for hours. Short-legged breeds are not as well suited for long hikes over rugged terrain.

Spitz Dogs

The plush coats of the smallest to the largest of this wolf-looking breed type indicates northern origins. The smaller breeds were bred to be companions.

Breed examples: Alaskan malamute, Siberian husky, chow chow, Pomeranian.

Positive hiking traits: Well-balanced physical proportions also found in natural or primitive dogs, alert, active. The larger breeds have good endurance and are happiest when working. Carrying dog packs is a good substitute for pulling a sled or a cart.

Concerns: Thick coats make many breeds vulnerable to overheating and restrict hiking to cooler high-country or winter conditions.

Terriers

Bred to track, tunnel out, and kill ground burrowing mammals (rats, badgers, rabbits, foxes). They evolved from the hounds.

Breed examples: Scottish terrier, American pit bull terrier, and dachshund.

Positive hiking traits: Robust, energetic. Some terriers have wiry coats that give them extra protection around dry, prickly brush.

Concerns: Some terriers can be belligerent around other dogs. Firm handling and obedience training are necessary.

Gun Dogs

Bred to find and retrieve game. Cooperation and responsiveness are two of the most valued traits in gun dogs, which also make them popular family dogs.

Breed examples: Labrador retriever, golden retriever, standard poodle, weimaraner, Brittany.

Positive hiking traits: Vigorous, generally gregarious, and easy to train. Dog breeds from this group display the best blend of desirable temperament and physical characteristics for the trail.

Concerns: If you are drawn to one of the very popular breeds like the Labradors and goldens, be very selective of the breeder. Sudden or extreme popularity of a breed often encourages indiscriminate breeding, which can result in an increase of physical and behavioral problems in some bloodlines.

Livestock

This working group was bred to primarily protect and/or herd the sheep, goats, and cattle with which they were raised.

Some breeds are being successfully trained to transfer their guarding instincts to provide personal protection.

Breed examples: German shepherd, boxer, rottweiler, mastiff, Australian shepherd, Old English sheepdog, Bernese.

Positive hiking traits: Herders of small to medium size are enthusiastic, athletic, outdoors-loving dogs that thrive on activity.

Concerns: The giant breeds, many used for draft or guard work in the mountains, have endurance but many may be afflicted with joint and bone problems that make them poor candidates for uphill hiking. Dogs bred for protection tend to have enhanced dominance. A hiker with such a dog should not be on the trail until the two have enough obedience training under their collar. You should be confident of your dog's reliability and of having the dog under control.

Companion

These dogs were originally and some more recently bred to be kept as family companions.

Breed examples: bichon frise, pug, poodles (toy, miniature and medium), cockapoo, dalmatian.

Positive hiking traits: This group is the most diverse in physical appearance and disposition, which makes generalizing difficult. As long as you are realistic about the dog's physical abilities and limitations, a well-mannered dog that is a good companion at home can be trained to become a good companion on the trail. In fact, the dainty looking papillon is actually one of the most physically fit breeds and its toy size gives it the advantage of being portable when necessary.

Concerns: Small dogs should be kept close to their owner on or off the leash in the woods to protect them from flying as well as stalking predators. In wild areas, golden eagles and other predators have been known to prey on smaller dogs.

SELECTING A DOG

Consider size, build, stamina, and temperament in selecting a dog for hiking; however, your selection should be made in conjunction with your personality and lifestyle off the trail. To reduce the chances of making an impulsive and less than perfect choice, decide what you need in a dog, then start looking. Ask yourself the following questions to determine your needs:

- Do you have children?
- Do you have indoor space for a small, medium, or large dog?
- Do you have a fenced yard? Tying a dog to a chain is cruel and promotes aggressive behavior.
- Do you have time to train and care for a hiking dog, and meet the dog's needs for exercise and mental stimulation off the trail?
- Do you have access to a park or natural area where your dog can romp, maintain his hiking form, and beat the boredom between hikes?
- Do you have time or the budget for dogs with high-maintenance grooming requirements?
- Do you have allergies? Pick a breed that does not shed.

GET PROFESSIONAL INPUT

Veterinarians, handlers, breeders, trainers, and groomers can give you valuable information during your quest for the ideal hiking dog. Also check the library and bookstore for books and magazines about dogs.

WHERE TO LOOK

Once you have narrowed down the breed for the best match, where do you find that future hiking companion?

Breeders: If you want a purebred, interview breeders. Word of mouth is the best source for a reputable breeder. The right breeder will be concerned with a good match between dog and owner rather than a fast buck. He will interview you carefully and forthrightly. That breeder will keep puppies for about 8 weeks, providing them with human companionship and regular exposure to household activity. The whelping or doggie nursery area should be clean, comfortable, and reflect that the breeder cares about the animals. Ask to meet the pup's mother, as her appearance and disposition will tell you a lot about the puppies. If the male is not available, ask to talk to his owner and veterinarian.

Breed rescue clubs: Many breed clubs have a rescue network for their own breed. The network is a support system for dog owners who are no longer able to keep the dog generally because of a change in personal circumstances. This can be a good source for someone who wants to bypass the trials and tribulations of puppy chewing and housebreaking by adopting a mature dog that may even have had extensive training.

Animal shelters: Visit your community animal shelter. Many wonderful purebreds and an even greater number of mixed breeds of different ages that deserve a good home are abandoned, lost, or given up to shelters daily. Some mixed breeds benefit from natural selection and display the best traits of their breed potpourri. If you find a dog that sparks your interest, get as much information as you can about the dog's breed or mix, background, and the reason the dog was given up for adoption. Talk to the shelter caretakers about their observations. Take the dog outside away from the chaos and stress of the shelter environment to interact with him and evaluate his disposition and your chemistry with him.

THE MORE THE MERRIER?

Two puppies are twice as cute and entertaining but double the trouble. Yes, they will keep each other company; however, they will be partners in crime, bonding to each other, rather than you, making them much less responsive to training. Instead of getting two puppies at the same time, bringing a second dog into the household when the first is an adult (at least 2 years old) and well trained, can be a lot of fun at home and on the trail. It is unnatural and cruel for dogs to spend their days alone. Their emotional well-being requires companionship. Adult dogs can be great teachers to pups.

A WORD ABOUT HYBRIDS

Hybrids are the result of any of various breeds of dog that have been crossbred with a wild canine (often a wolf). Although there are laws in many states prohibiting ownership of a hybrid along with many reasons not to own one, people are often seduced by a hybrid's wild beauty. However, the look is not always all that is wild. Whereas some domesticated dogs are a challenge, hybrids are often unmanageable. Your dog's wild instincts at some point will override socialization, domestication, and training. Speaking strictly of trail circumstances, he will be torn between loyalty to you and resisting unadulterated urges to chase prey. A hybrid breed from a dog with strong guarding instincts (e.g., German shepherd) compounds the problem. Even on a leash, passing hikers with other dogs on the narrow trails will be a challenge of control with an instinctively territorial dog.

The best match between dog and owner stems from picking a dog you love and being aware of his needs.

3

Bonding

Bonding is the loyalty, trust, and cooperation between you and your dog. A solid bond is crucial to successful training and fosters reliability on the trail. Bonding makes dogs more prone to please and therefore more likely to respond to commands.

EARLY BONDING

There can be variations in bonding by breed and individuals. It is generally accepted that most puppies need to be with their mother until about seven or eight weeks of age. The learning that occurs between mother and pup is one of the building blocks for a well-adjusted dog.

Puppies that engage in regular interactive play are smarter and easily settle in their slot of the pecking order because they have had plenty of opportunity to practice their social and communication skills. Dogs that are removed from the litter too young or isolated from other dogs during this phase can later display excessive timidity or unprovoked aggression around other dogs.

Six to eight weeks is the peak time for human attachments when pups need to be frequently handled by humans. Introduce pups to new experiences, which makes future training easier.

Affection reinforces the bond between dog and owner

PLAY

A dog's first bonding experience and lessons in social behavior come through physical and mental play with her littermates. In addition to being a good bonding tool, play promotes social skills, agility, and resourcefulness. A hike can be a shared playtime between you and your dog. Experts warn against engaging in play fighting with your dog during the socialization period when you could be reinforcing dominance traits that could develop into aggression problems later on.

MATURE BONDING

After six to eight weeks, bonding occurs through consistent pleasurable interaction, including physical touch (from petting to massaging), feeding, walking, playing, training, and positive reinforcement of desired behavior through rewards (verbal praise, stroking, and treats). The more timid the dog the more time, patience, and constant reassurance are required to nurture it to some state of trust.

A dog regularly isolated in the yard, kennel, or separate room can feel ostracized. Dogs need to be integrated in the daily activities of their human pack as much as possible. Hiking and backpacking excursions provide excellent opportunities for quality bonding time.

FOOD

Food is another way to a dog's heart. Dogs bond more readily to a hand that feeds them. In the case of a shy dog, begin by hand feeding a few bites before putting the food bowl down. Dogs are always enthusiastic about the humans who give them treats and throw tennis balls.

Nurturing the bond between you and your dog from the very beginning is the glue that will keep your dog responsive to training.

4

Obedience

One of the gratifying aspects of obedience classes and hiking is that they complement each other. The drills prepare your dog, and the trail becomes an arena to practice and reinforce classroom lessons. Obedience is especially important for a hiking dog because the nuisance and hazard of a few uncontrolled dogs can result in all dogs being banned them the trail.

DOES YOUR DOG NEED OBEDIENCE TRAINING?

If the fact that basic obedience facilitates and enhances your relationship with your dog isn't motivation enough, realize that once you step out of your yard and onto the trail everything your dog is and isn't reflects on you and impacts other people, animals, and the surrounding environment. Basic obedience skills are essential on the trail.

Two vital aspects of your dog's trail education include:

- Learning appropriate behavior around the people and animals on the trail.
- Learning to respond to commands in spite of the naturally seductive sights, sounds, and smells of the trail. Your dog's repertoire of commands should at least include come, sit, down, stay, and heel, no, and leave it.

A well-trained dog will avoid the instinctive impulse to chase wildlife.

TRAINING OPTIONS

You can train your dog yourself; there are several good training books on the market or at your local library (see Appendix D). The two main advantages of training your dog on your own are control of the training schedule and the minimal cost. The "doing it yourself method" works best if you know and understand how a dog thinks and have the self-discipline to set aside 15 minutes twice a day to work with your dog.

Successful training is not measured just by the achievement of a dog's sitting, staying, and coming. The objective is to have your dog respond to a command with respectful but enthusiastic immediacy, rather than cowering compliance. Be careful with your dog's psyche. Remember, calling your dog over to give her a reprimand is as counterproductive to fostering reliable off-leash recalls as sticking your pup's nose in her business is to housebreaking.

You might opt to enroll your dog in a group obedience class or hire a private trainer. In teaching your dog commands for the trail, tone and verbal and body language can give mixed or vague messages that confuse the animal, frustrate the owner, and undermine hiker/dog team spirit.

A good trainer quickly gets the desired response from a dog (sitting, lying down, heeling) and can teach all the necessary commands your pet needs to be a good citizen. The secret to controlling a dog is to communicate clearly, confidently, and in some cases, assertively.

Qualified trainers can help you work with and around your dog's natural instincts and breed characteristics, so that traits like dominance, guarding instincts, chasing, stealing, independence, hyperalertness, opportunism, or roaming do not become problems. Trainers can also instruct you in the appropriate use of tools such as choke collars.

Group classes cost only a reasonable fee through local kennel clubs, pet supply stores, and veterinary clinics. Consider enrolling in a puppy class or adult obedience class as an investment in your dog's and your relationship on the trail. Regardless of whether you are an experienced or first-time dog owner, the controlled but buzzing environment of a group class makes an excellent training ground for dogs to work on their social interaction with other dogs and humans while learning to ignore distractions.

HOW SOON SHOULD YOU START TRAINING YOUR DOG?

Although dogs are not admitted to puppy classes until they have had at least their first two DHLP-P (distemper/parvo) vaccinations at about 10 weeks, you should start working with your puppy on your own.

Basic training should start from the time the pup is born. Puppies that are handled by human hands early on bond more easily and accept human touch more readily. Practice calling your puppy enthusiastically to come and rewarding him with praise, petting, and a treat. This is the first step in many months of work toward every dog owner's ultimate goal—a reliable recall off leash. Never use your dog's name to reprimand, punish, or administer anything your dog views as unpleasant. The more pleasant the experience, the more reason to come quickly when you call his name.

Responsible owners with well-trained dogs will be more confident and relaxed as they enjoy their dog's companionship in nature.

5

Training Tips and Tools

In nature, social order is essential for survival. It determines who breeds, leads, cares for the young, guards, and who eats when. Providing the alpha leader for your dog's pack will play on his instincts and he will be more responsive, calmer, happier, and better integrated in the family if his position in the pack is reaffirmed. The hiking dog learns to respect you as the leader both on and off the trail.

THE IMPORTANCE OF BEING CONSISTENT

Inconsistency breeds unpredictability. Rules and routine should be the same on the trail as they are at home. No should mean no, anywhere. You do not want her testing you on the trail, where a rebellious act could put her life at risk or jeopardize someone else's safety.

Potty-Training for the Trail

Conditioning your dog to relieve himself on command on leash is a housebreaking method that proves a valuable habit at roadside rest stops on the way to the trailhead or anytime you may need to monitor where your dog relieves himself during the hike. Begin at home by taking your dog outside on a leash at routine elimination times and use a short command phrase like "hurry up" or any comfortable expression (English or foreign language). Use the expression as your dog relieves himself, avoiding an overzealous tone that could distract him from business. Reward your dog with a pat, enthusiastic praise, and a treat.

CRATE TRAINING

If used appropriately, a crate can be one of the most valuable training tools you will ever own. Molded plastic airline-approved crates with side ventilation and a metal grate door with a latch have the most flexibility. They can be purchased at most airports from the airline, pet supply stores, or from pet supply catalogs. This type is useful for housebreaking, easy to clean, and safe for transporting your dog in a vehicle and on airplanes. In all probability, your dog will eventually

Proper training makes the crate a comfortable retreat

experience the crate at the veterinarian or the groomer, so it is a good idea to familiarize her with it as soon as possible. For young or old dogs, the principles of crate training are the same.

What Size?

The crate should be large enough for the dog to lie, sit, stand, and move around comfortably with enough space for bedding (soft blanket or towel), a couple of toys, and a food and water dish. If you own a large breed, expect to upgrade the size of the crate at least once during the pup's growing months. Be aware that the airline will not let your dog aboard in an inadequate crate. You will be required to have a larger or more appropriate crate on site or miss your flight.

Four Steps to Successful Crate Training

The goal is to help your dog think of the crate as a den, a safe, clean comfortable place where he feels relaxed and content, not incarcerated.

1. The crate should always be kept where your dog can feel like part of the family. Remember that dogs are social animals and isolation from the family in the laundry room, the garage, or the yard makes them feel like they are being ostracized from the "pack" and punished. Between six and eight weeks, pups should sleep next to their owner's bed (in the crate).

2. Initially place the crate with door open, wherever he is most likely to investigate it.

3. After a good play session and a romp outside to relieve himself, encourage your dog to explore the inside of the

crate where he'll find his blanket, toys, treats, and whatever particulars make the crate a pleasant place.

4. Place your dog's food dish at the back of the crate and feed one or two meals a day in the crate with the door open for about a week or until your dog is comfortable entering and leaving the crate. Later close the door for a short while, gradually increasing your dog's time in the crate.

Pups less than four months should not be left alone or in the crate more than two hours at a time. On the road, dogs of any age should be taken out of the crate at least every couple of hours.

PACK TRAINING

Begin by placing a face cloth or small towel on your dog's back to introduce your dog to the feel of weight on his back. Leave the pack around the house near his bed or crate for a few days and in the car when you take him for a ride.

Feed him little treats while you try the pack on (empty) and praise him for having the pack on. Take it off and repeat the exercise twice a day for about a week.

The next step is to put the pack on for going on a leash walk. Give him the treat while you are putting the pack on and then put his leash on as you would on a regular walk.

Put the pack on for short hikes with only treats in the pouches, so you can take the treats from his pack on snack breaks. The idea is to create positive associations with the pack so that eventually the sight of the pack evokes an enthusiastic response from your dog.

ANTIBARK COLLARS

A barking dog is an intrusion in nature. If barking is going to be a problem, consider a citronella spray antibark collar—it is more humane than a traditional shock collar. Barking triggers the release of a burst of lemon-scented spray under her nose. The unpleasant and startling spray eliminates barking with most dogs. (Collars and refills are available at veterinary behavior clinics, trainers, some pet stores, and mail-order catalogs.)

Getting to the trail safely

Maybe traveling has not been part of your dog's lifestyle until now, but chances are your hiking excursions will involve some vehicle travel time. Ideally, your vehicle should be large enough to accommodate a dog crate or a dog barrier so both dog and passengers are safe and comfortable. Dogs hopping between the front and back seats are a distraction and hazard to the driver, and dogs bouncing in the bed of pickup trucks are at risk of serious injury.

- Never put the crate or the dog in direct sunlight.
- Provide adequate ventilation and remember that in the summertime, cracking the window is *never* enough, even on a cloudy day. Dogs die in overheated cars, even during short stops.
- Offer your dog water at every stop.
- Train yourself to leash him before you open the car door.
- Train him to "wait" or "stay" in the crate or in the vehicle until you issue a command like "okay" or "hop out." These communication cues can save your dog's life.

All aboard

Initially the vehicle should be stationary in the garage or driveway; turn the engine on and sit for a few times. Next take a short drive down the street with a stop for a walk or a play session to promote the positive association with the car ride. Getting in the car only for veterinarian visits is a sure way to sabotage your road training efforts.

Once you feel confident that your dog is comfortable riding in the car, take her with you around town as often as you can: stop at a park for a walk or even stroll through your local pet supply store for a biscuit. Drive smoothly, avoid winding roads, and gradually increase the length of the drives between routine stops.

Remember to make frequent stops for stretching and sniffing on longer road trips, and offer her water at every stop.

Motion Sickness

Dogs prone to motion sickness should not be fed on the morning of the drive; instead, feed them an hour after arrival or when they seem recovered from the stress of the drive. Food and hyperventilation can be an uncomfortable and dangerous combination, especially for large breeds with a predisposition to bloating.

Consult your veterinarian about the appropriate use of Dramamine to treat motion sickness and certain antihistamines for their calming effects as opposed to medications that sedate.

Cool Ride

Make your dog more comfortable during a hot drive to and from the trailhead by covering his bedding with a wet towel. Water-absorbent crate mats are available through mail-order catalogs. Never leave your pet unattended in a vehicle for mor that a very few minutes. Even with a window cracked, your car can become a deadly oven.

6

Conditioning Your Dog

Preparing your dog for hiking is like coaching an athlete for an Olympic decathlon. You must get her in good physical condition (muscular and cardiovascular) to enjoy the hike safely. Certain parts of your dog's body will require special care and attention before hiking to prevent injury or discomfort. Mental conditioning includes familiarizing her with hiking equipment and the trail environment.

PREHIKE CARE

Dewclaws: All dogs are born with front dewclaws, and many have rear dewclaws. This fifth digit on the inside of the leg is prone to tearing and ideally should be removed by a veterinarian within a few days after birth. If dewclaws have not been removed, consider having this surgery done at the same time your dog is spayed or neutered.

Nails: Nails should be short without sacrificing traction. Even dogs that are active enough outdoors to keep their nails naturally worn need to have the nail on the dewclaw trimmed. Consult a groomer or your veterinarian on the proper use of dog nail clippers and nail file for maintenance between clips.

Feet: Dog footpads get toughened (light sandpaper texture) by regular and gradual extended walks and runs on rough and varied surfaces (pavement, sand, or rocks). Booties should be worn to alleviate tenderness and protect footpads from cuts on ice and sharp rocks.

Spaying and neutering: Your dog will be just as smart, loving, and trim after it is altered—altering does not make them fat, too much food and too little exercise do. Besides some of the social and medical benefits of altering, which include a reduced incidence of mammary gland cancer in females and prostate cancer in males, a decreased sexual drive will make your pet less apt to roam or tangle with other dogs. The trail advantage of neutering is a male that is more congenial and less preoccupied with competition around other males.

Vaccinations: Your dog should be current on all vaccinations (DHLP-P, rabies, and a vaccination against Lyme disease are advisable).

Heartworm: Mosquitoes carry this parasite. Consult your veterinarian about heartworm preventive medication.

Fleas and ticks: Dogs can be infected with tapeworm by ingesting fleas that are carriers of tapeworm eggs. Some types of ticks are carriers of disease (see Chapter 9). There is a bigger arsenal of flea and tick products on the market than ever. Consult your veterinarian on a treatment for your dog and his hiking needs.

Grooming: Long coats should be trimmed (not shaved), particularly under the belly and behind the legs during the summer. Trimming hair between the toes prevents foxtails (invasive grasses found primarily in the western U.S.) from going undetected while they burrow, puncture, and infect. In the winter, less hair between the toes prevents the formation of icicles around the pads, decreasing the chance for frostbite.

BUILDING CONFIDENCE

Exposure to the trail at an early age (preferably before 12 weeks) will help build your dog's confidence. Dogs get comfortable with sounds, sights, and experiences by early and constant exposure as pups (ideally before 16 weeks old). Beyond four months of age, new experiences are met with a degree of natural apprehension and caution. If your dog has already developed a fear of certain situations, you will need to recondition her by introducing the threatening stimuli gradually and in small doses. This is often typical of the more primitive breeds and particularly hybrids, whose acute survival instincts prevent them from taking the new and unusual in stride.

On the other hand, this environmental hyperawareness can become an asset on the trail. Such a dog may sense and communicate real dangers to you before you even see, hear, or feel the hint of a threat. He may be the one to smell or see the bear, hear the landslide, or feel a precarious situation developing.

TRAIL SIGHTS

Let your dog get used to seeing backpacks, walking sticks, tents, and other hiking equipment around the house. Simulate trail circumstances by having friends with backpacks, walking sticks, and fishing rods stroll around the yard or come around the corner while you are on a walk with your dog. By the time you head for the trail, strangers waddling toward your dog in full backcountry outfits will not cause retreat or barking. There may be horses, pack stock, and cyclists on the trail, so introduce your canine companion to these ahead of time.

BUILDING STAMINA

Puppies Eight-Sixteen Weeks Old

Even a big backyard can be full of adventures and exploration possibilities for a pup. It is a good idea to introduce your pup to the natural hiking setting as early as possible, but you must be sensible about her vulnerability to infectious diseases. Pups get their initial immunity from their mother's milk, but they need protection through inoculation after they stop nursing.

By 12 weeks, your pup should have had the first of three DHLP-P vaccinations. Although it may be reasonably safe to socialize and romp around other pups on the same vaccination schedule, hold off on the great outdoors until she has had her final series of DHLP-P and rabies vaccination (four to six months). Try to take her to a park, beach, or neighborhood trail for exercise and sensory stimulation (20- to 30-minute sessions) in addition to playtime and at least two leash walks daily. Use good sense and do not expose your pup to strange dogs or other animals until she has been vaccinated against rabies.

Puppies Four-Six Months Old

By now your puppy should be fully immunized and can safely venture away from the grassy green belts of civilization and closer to nature. Fields, meadows, or nearby forested trails will be more stimulating for your puppy, although the distractions will make training more challenging for both of you.

Use a long rope or expandable leash (20 to 30 feet) so your pup can romp and explore under controlled conditions. Practice "sit," "stay," "down," and "come" at the end of the rope several times. Let him off in a safe area of the trail and practice calling him enthusiastically during these prehike drills, rewarding him with a "good dog," a pat, and treat tidbits. Always use verbal praise and a pat, and when the desired behavior becomes consistent, use food rewards only some of the time.

Tell your dog to go play and do not call him unless you have eye contact or know you have his attention. When he is busy smelling, listening, or digging for creatures, he does not hear you. Do not compete and set yourselves up for failure. Never call him to you for a reprimand no matter how frustrated you may be with his behavior.

These introductory training excursions (30 minutes to one hour) will leave an overactive puppy calm and sleepy for his indoor life. Remember that during the first several months (6 for small dogs, 9 to 12 for larger dogs), most of the dog's energy is going into the growth of his young body. Do not stress the healthy development of your dog's muscles and bones with long distances and hills. With giant breeds, until 12 to 18 months keep the excursions short (under one hour) and on mostly flat terrain.

Take frequent rest stops and water breaks. In warm weather, stop every 20 minutes for your puppy to rest and drink water.

Adult Dogs

Gradual conditioning principles also apply to adult dogs that are just being introduced to the fun of hiking. If your dog's arena of physical activity has been primarily in the yard, begin by planning a walking route that allows you to be out 30 minutes twice daily (morning and evening). Following is an example of a 5-week training program that can be adapted to your lifestyle and your dog's fitness level. Consult your physician and your veterinarian before making any changes to your and your dog's physical activity level.

The suggested longer walk at the end of week 5 is about increasing distance, not speed. Consider using this week 5 as a guideline for maintaining your dog's conditioning between hikes.

Once you both feel reasonably fit, incorporate some stairs or a hill to train for the up and down of backcountry

Week 1 Morning and Evening	15-minute sniff and stroll (warm-up) 10-minute brisk walk (cardiovascular workout) 5-minute sniff and stroll (cool-down)
Week 2 Morning and Evening	15-minute sniff and stroll (warm-up) 20-minute brisk walk (cardiovascular workout) 5-minute sniff and stroll (cool-down)
Week 3 Morning and Evening	15-minute sniff and stroll (warm-up) 20-minute brisk walk (cardiovascular workout) 5-minute sniff and stroll (cool-down)
Week 4 Morning and Evening	15-minute sniff and stroll (warm-up) 30-minute brisk walk (cardiovascular workout) 10-minute stroll and sniff (cool-down)
Week 5 Morning and Evening	15-minute sniffing and stopping (warm-up) 30-minute brisk walk (cardiovascular workout) 10-minute stroll and sniff (cool-down) Plus one additional longer walk at end of week (about 1.5 hours)

trails. Ideally, your dog should be getting at least two hours of outdoor exercise daily including walks and off-leash playtime. Make sure she always has drinking water, shade, and rest as needed.

During the summer months, shade from trees or cooling off in surface water helps dogs regulate their body temperature. If your dog decides to lounge in a mud puddle, let her. A dirty dog is the least of your worries (see Chapter 9).

PACING

A person of average physical fitness walks about 3 miles per hour on a paved level path. To get a better idea of your and your dog's average stride and pace, time yourself walking around the local high school running track with him on leash (tracks are 0.25 mile per lap). Keep in mind that on a hike, the terrain, weather, elevation, and steep climbs will affect your pace. In the mountains, for every 1,000 feet of elevation gain, you can add one extra mile to the original length of the hike. Contrary to what many people think, hiking downhill is not twice as fast as hiking uphill. It takes about three-quarters of the time to hike the same distance downhill.

HEALTH CONSIDERATIONS

Seriously and realistically consider your dog's age and current physical condition. This is not to say that if your dog is older, overweight, or has a medical condition, she cannot hike. But if common sense precludes a human couch potato from sprinting a mile or driving to 8,000 feet for a 5-mile hike, the same applies to a dog who spends most of her life between the yard and her dog bed.

Consult your veterinarian to help evaluate your pet's health and discuss under what conditions hiking would be beneficial.

7

Day Hike Gear

There are certain necessary items to make your day hikes with your dog safe and more enjoyable. The following list describes gear options that can further increase your and your dog's safety and enhance your hiking experience. Many of the day hike equipment items are essential building blocks to a successful backpacking excursion (Chapter 8).

COLLARS AND HARNESSES

Either a collar or harness is suitable, but a colorful harness makes your dog more visible and identifies him as domestic. For dogs of intimidating size or appearance, a colorful harness emphasizes their pet status. It is easier to restrain a dog by a harness than a collar when necessary. In addition, a harness is a safer restraint (a collar could slip off or choke the animal) if your dog were ever in a predicament requiring you to pull him out of water or hoist him up a hillside.

Fabric: Although leather is the most durable, nylon collars and harnesses are available in vibrant colors, are usually adjustable, and dry more quickly and without shrinkage.

Fit: You should be able to easily slip your flat hand under the collar and rotate the collar; however, it should not be so loose that it can slip over the dog's head. A puppy will need to be fitted with a new collar a couple of times as he grows. Harnesses need to fit loosely enough to allow full expansion of the chest and a free stride. Never use a choke collar as a permanent collar. Dogs wearing choke collars off leash have been known to suffer serious injuries and death. Strangulation has occurred when another dog's jaw was twisted in the choke collar during rambunctious play.

IDENTIFICATION TAGS

On the trail a tag is the most obvious way to reunite a lost pet and its owner. The information should include the dog's name (first and last name), telephone number with area code, and street address (not a P.O. box). The sight, smell, or sound of another animal could lure your dog away, and thunder or gunshots have startled dogs to run off. Whatever the reason for the separation, you want to facilitate the reunion. If another person gets close enough to your dog to see the tag, the first thing he or she will look for is a name. Calling the dog by its name will establish some communication and trust. The telephone number allows the finder to leave a message with someone in your household or on your answering machine.

Temporary identification: In addition to her permanent tag, your dog needs a temporary identification tag when you are hiking out of town. The tag should have the date and the telephone number of where you are staying (campground, friend's house, or hotel). If you are on a day hike, write the name of the trail, your destination, and the trailhead where you are parked. Check with the ranger station for messages.

Securing the tag: Loop rings are more secure than S rings for attaching tags. Small plastic luggage tags on a loop ring make inexpensive reusable temporary tags.

LEASHES

A leash that will suffer the abuse of the trail (rain, rocks, streams, and snow) must be durable. On the one hand, colored nylon webbed leash is light, dries quickly, and is easy to spot when you lay it down. You can design your own leash inexpensively by buying the webbed nylon by the foot at a mountaineering store and the clasp at a hardware store.

On the other hand, leather leashes stay the cleanest and last forever. Place a piece of colored tape or tie a strand of colored fabric to the handle to make finding the leash easier when it is on the ground. Leather leashes are usually required in most obedience classes.

If you are hiking in a strictly on-leash environment, expandable leashes blend control and freedom. The leashes come in varied lengths and strengths based on dog weight. An expandable leash can also convert into a tie-out line.

BANDANNAS

A colorful bandanna around a dog's neck sends two important messages. It can say "cute," which helps make big dogs

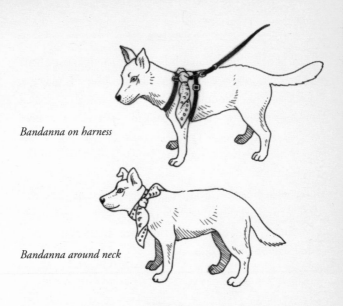

Bandanna on harness

Bandanna around neck

look less intimidating to those hikers who may be fearful of them. In the forest, a bright bandanna says "domestic," which helps distinguish dogs from game during the hunting season. For extra visibility, tie the bandanna on a colorful harness.

REFLECTIVE VEST

If you are going to hike during hunting season, your dog should wear a bright lightweight reflective vest, designed for sporting dogs. Hunters are familiar with reflective vests, which further distinguish your dog from wildlife.

BOOTIES

If your pet is an occasional hiker who spends most of his time sauntering across the lawn at home, his pads may get tender even after a couple of miles. Booties can give relief to your dog's sore paws until his pads toughen as well as prevent cuts from crusty or icy trail conditions. Your dog should practice wearing booties at home before trying them on the trail.

Where to buy booties: Booties come in different sizes and materials and are available through pet supply stores, mail-order catalogs, and mountaineering stores and are advertised in dog sledding magazines.

Booties help protect tender paws

DOG PACKS

Although it is a good idea to introduce young dogs to the idea of packs, loaded packs should be used only on adult, medium to large dogs (35 pounds or more).

Most packs are designed to lie on the dog's back like a saddle with a pouch on each side. Packs are more appropriate for backpacking than day hikes. There's significantly more gear when you go overnight and it's a good use of dog power to train a medium- or large-size dog to assist by carrying her booties, first-aid kit, food, and treats or other accessories related to her needs.

Choosing packs: Packs are sold in pet supply stores, outdoor recreation stores, and pet mail-order catalogs. They come in different sizes with adjustable straps. Look for the design that best conforms to your dog's body. The pack should feature breathable material, rounded corners, and padding for additional comfort.

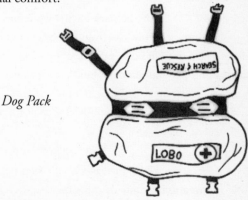

Dog Pack

Packs should conform to your dog's build

Pack fitting: Your dog's comfort depends on a proper fit. The pack sits on his shoulders between the base of the neck and short of the hips. There should be one strap that clips on his chest and one or two belly straps to stabilize the pack. Straps should be tight enough to keep the pack in place but loose enough to allow full stride without chafing and comfortable expansion of the chest for breathing.

Loading the packs: Stuff the packs with newspaper at first, then gradually increase the load from 10 percent of his weight not to exceed a third of his weight, once he is accustomed to the packs and his endurance is built up. If you use packs only occasionally, keep the weight on the lighter side—it should be equal and evenly distributed so as not to interfere with your dog's balance.

Pack safety: Keep your dog on leash when he is wearing his packs. Packs can make balance awkward when negotiating narrow mountainside trails or crossing fast streams. Give him a break every hour or so by removing the packs so he enjoys the freedom you both came for by playing, swimming, and rolling around without risking injury to himself and damage to his packs and cargo. Remember, the weight of packs should not exceed a third of a dog's weight.

LIFE VEST

A life vest is important to have if you are going to hike near rivers and lakes or if you have to cross high water especially with dogs who are drawn to water. An elderly or tired dog is more at risk in the water during a hike than she would be at the beach for the day.

FLASHLIGHT AND EXTRA BATTERIES

You will be thankful for a flashlight if you are still hiking after sunset, especially one that fits in a day pack.

MATCHES AND CIGARETTE LIGHTER

Temperatures can drop quickly after the sun goes down. If you are lost or injured, a fire can help keep you warm until daylight or help arrives. Put matches and a strike strip in a pill bottle to protect them from the elements.

LIGHTWEIGHT NYLON TARP

In an emergency, a tarp makes a lightweight shelter from sun, wind, and rain. Purchase a lightweight plastic one at a local hardware or outdoor store.

FLYERS FOR A LOST DOG

Carry a few photocopied flyers with your dog's photo, name, description of area where he was lost (name of trail), and a contact number. Post a flyer at the trailhead, campground, and ranger station, and carry one that you can show other hikers along the way.

FOOD

Dogs require a balanced diet made up of five essential nutrients: protein, fat, carbohydrates, minerals, and vitamins.

Types of Food

Human food (cooked poultry, meat, and rice) is tasty and freshest but requires more preparation and planning. Commercial dog food comes moist (canned), semimoist (sealed pouches), and dry. Premium brands sold at supermarkets and pet supply stores provide balanced diets. Dogs with restricted diets due to medical conditions are often fed "prescription" brands obtained from a veterinarian.

How Much Do I Feed My Dog?

Puppies are generally fed three or four smaller meals and adults one or two large meals per day. Some dog owners find it more convenient to feed adult dogs once a day, although dividing their daily portion into two smaller meals (morning and evening) is more desirable, especially with hiking dogs. Exercising on a full stomach is uncomfortable because most of the blood supply of the body is occupied with digestion rather than supplying oxygen to the muscles and the cardiovascular system. Be aware that some breeds are more sensitive to bloating, and eating large amounts before exercising can compound the risks.

It is not necessary to increase your dog's amount of food for a day hike. Instead supplement his diet at snack breaks. Pack dog biscuits, jerky treats, and a pouch of semi-moist food or extra dry kibbles.

In cold weather, think of taking along higher-protein dog snacks (see Appendix B and Chapter 8 for backpacking feeding tips).

PLASTIC RESEALABLE BAGS

This airtight, self-sealing invention is in the top five essentials for the trail. They are great for carrying food and treats, medication, and first-aid necessities and can easily be converted into food and water bowls. Their sealing quality comes in handy for disposing of dog waste.

WATER

Water is as essential to your dog as it is to you. Do not count on finding water along the trail. Dehydration can result in sluggishness, kidney problems, and heat stroke. Both humans and dogs are vulnerable to dehydration in the heat and at high elevations.

Do not let your dog drink from standing water in puddles, ponds, lakes, or swimming holes in slow-moving creeks and rivers. That's where different forms of bacteria and algae breed, and small dogs and puppies have been known to get very ill and in some cases die from drinking contaminated water. Be especially wary of areas where cattle graze. Both dogs and humans are susceptible to the intestinal parasite *Giardia lamblia*, which can cause cramping and diarrhea, leading to serious dehydration. *Giardia* can be present in all sources of untreated water.

How Much Water Do I Need?

Carry at least 8 ounces of water per dog per hour of hiking. Consider that an average walking pace on level ground is about 3 miles per hour. Fill plastic water bottles (three-quarters full) and place in the freezer the night before. Your dog will have a source of cool fresh water as the ice melts along the way. Two frozen water bottles can also serve to keep her cooler by placing one in each pouch of her dog pack.

Offer your dog water frequently (every half hour or more on hot days). It is easier to regulate hydration with regular small intakes of water.

Snow may keep your dog cool, but do not believe a hot, thirsty dog will instinctively know to eat snow to quench her thirst. One hiker reported that her Southern California born and raised dog was almost delirious from dehydration after taking him on a summer hike up a mountain where she thought the abundant snow would make up for the lack of water.

BOWLS

Weight and encumbrances are the main concerns when packing for a hike. There are plenty of ways to create inexpensive doggie dinnerware on the trail. Paper or plastic picnic plates and bowls are lightweight and adequate for food and water. A plastic zip-locked bag can store the kibble and convert into a food dish or water bowl (hold the bag while your dog drinks from it). Pet supply stores and mail-order catalogs have several doggie gadgets for carrying and serving food and water on the trail, from canteens to collapsible bowls.

FIRST-AID KIT

Although you cannot prepare for all the mishaps, it is best to have a few first-aid items. You can add doggy items to your regular first-aid kit (see Appendix A for a dog first-aid kit checklist).

See Appendix A for a more detailed checklist of day hiking gear.

8

Backpacking Gear

Maybe it's the thought of retreating deeper into the solitary beauty of the wilderness with your four-legged companion that draws you. Or perhaps you're satisfied with setting up camp a few miles up the trailhead to share an easy idyllic overnight in the great outdoors with him. Whichever appeals to you, backpacking with your dog requires some extra necessities and additional planning. Your goal is to travel light while considering emergencies, outdoor dining pleasures, and sleeping comforts for both you and your dog. Refer to checklists in Appendix A for basic gear discussions, but add the following things to your list for a backpacking adventure.

PERMITS

Permits are generally obtained from ranger stations of the government agency that manages the land you wish to hike (e.g., national or state park or forest, Bureau of Land Management). Permits are usually required for overnights in wilderness areas and in other heavily used recreation areas. In some places, registering or obtaining a permit can be required even for day hiking. In areas where use is strictly limited, you may have to apply for a permit several months ahead of time.

FOOD

Make a list of the number of meals and snacks per hiking day for you and your dog. Package his meals and snacks (preferably dry or semimoist) individually in zip-locked bags for convenience and to keep the food smells from attracting bears.

You can safely supplement your dog's dry kibbles with most human food you would bring for yourself, except sugar and chocolate (chocolate is toxic to dogs as well as cats). Plan to take one extra cup of human food per day to supplement your dog's dinner in camp. Pasta and rice are lightweight and easy to cook in camp and can be prepared creatively for extra taste and nutrition.

A little olive oil, garlic, onion, and zucchini go a long way to satisfy vegetarians. Meat eaters can add canned tuna or chicken as well as any freeze-dried meat sauce or soup mix. Either way, your dog will appreciate the added flavor to her kibbles and benefit from the energy fuel. Introduce her to new foods at home before going on the trail.

Cutting your dog's regular dog food with puppy food will add the extra protein and fat needed for the higher calorie-burning excursions. Begin mixing small amounts of puppy food about 3 days before the hike so your dog's digestive system can adapt gradually.

WATER

You need to take enough water for drinking (you and the dog) and cooking. If you are sure of the availability of water, consider carrying less and boiling, filtering, or chemically treating the water in camp. There are several water purification systems available at outdoor recreation stores, but be aware that some dogs will not drink chemically treated water.

BEDDING

For yourself, choose a sleeping bag rated to keep you warm in the region and season you are backpacking.

For your dog, carry a piece of foam and a towel rolled up with your sleeping bag. Lightweight dog bedrolls, designed

Comforts of Camp

to be cuddly on one side and durable on the side in contact with the ground are available in pet supply stores and mail-order catalogs.

If you choose to sleep under the stars, make sure your dog is staked on a line (6-foot radius from his stake or tree) short enough to keep him away from the campfire but long enough to have physical contact with you. Physical contact gives your dog the security that will help keep him quieter if the sounds of the dark outdoors are new to him, enables you to hush him at the first hint of a growl, keeps him warmer on cold nights, and lets you know when he's on alert.

SHELTER

A tent gives you more protection from the elements and the wilderness nightlife. Buy one that can accommodate your dog. As a guideline, some of the lightweight three-person dome tents are roomy enough to fit two medium-sized dogs as well. Dogs used to indoor creature comforts will want and should sleep in the tent. Even inside the tent, your dog will alert you to suspicious sounds and smells.

SETTING UP CAMP

Evening

1. Pick your campsite in daylight, taking into account exposure, water, mosquitoes, and your dog's comfort.
2. Put your dog on her tie-out line where she can curl up to rest, and give her water while you set up camp (sleeping and cooking quarters).

Collapsible bowl

Tie-out line

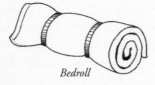

Bedroll

3. Get enough water to boil or filter for cooking dinner and breakfast, and enough drinking water for you and pooch for the evening and following trail day (8 ounces per mile per dog).

4. Prepare dinner for you and pooch.

5. Wash the dishes and burn or seal garbage in plastic bags for pack-out to remove any food smells from camp.

6. Walk your dog before bedtime, tidy up camp, and snuggle up for the night.

Morning

7. Walk the dog and clean up any of her waste.

8. Share a hot breakfast with her (instant hot cereal or scrambled eggs over her kibble, with a hot drink for you and warm water for her).

9. Clean up and pack up. Leave your campsite cleaner than you found it.

THREE REASONS WHY YOUR DOG SHOULD BE ATTENDED IN CAMP AT ALL TIMES

1. He will be vulnerable to wild predators.

2. It is unfair to cause him stress from being separated from you in unfamiliar surroundings.

3. Separation anxiety is often expressed through barking, whining, and howling, which ruins the wilderness experience for other campers. Do not forget that separation anxiety could bring on a chewing rampage that might leave you with a shredded tent, sleeping bag, or backpack.

With good planning and careful attention to gear, backpacking can heighten the pleasures of the trail for you and your dog.

For a detailed backpacking checklist, see Appendix A.

9

On the Trail

Every hike shares routine preparations but some destinations require more specific planning. In addition, the coast, mountains, desert, and forest offer different sources of enjoyment as well as challenges that can affect your dog.

GENERAL CONSIDERATIONS

Always get information ahead of time about the area where you want to hike. *Are dogs allowed?* Determine which agency regulates the area (national, state, regional, or other), call ahead for restrictions about dogs on the trails, and abide by the rules. *Do you need a permit?* Call the managing agency about its regulations.

What kind of weather can you expect? The high country is subject to variable and extreme weather. Check the weather forecast and fire danger advisory at a ranger station. Afternoon thunderstorms in the summer are common and it is best to be below timberline and off exposed ridges. In the spring and fall, pay attention to the sudden drops in temperature and clouds moving in that may announce snowfall.

What are the trail conditions? Advisories about fast water, high streams, and trail damage are commonly posted at a ranger station or visitor center. If nothing is posted, ask anyway.

What is the terrain like? A topographical map is an indispensable tool in planning your hike. Learn to read the information. A topographic map indicates boundaries between public lands and private lands and clearly shows marked trails and campgrounds. It shows you the elevation changes and how hilly or flat the surrounding terrain may be, so you can anticipate the difficulty of the trail and pace yourself appropriately. Every 1,000 feet of elevation equals about 1 extra mile of hiking. The map shows you if there is surface water (lakes, streams, and rivers) along the way. Studying the topographic map of the region beforehand allows you to choose the most appropriate trail for your dog's comfort and safety and to pack accordingly. Forests mean more shade; open ridge trails mean potential exposure to the elements (heat of the day, wind, and lightning); meadows mean mosquitoes; streams, rivers, and lakes indicate cooling stops.

What wildlife can you expect? You will want to know about bears, mountain lions, rattlesnakes, or other creatures that may be a safety concern to you and your dog.

What if something happens? Leave a copy of your itinerary with a friend or family member. Use his or her name and contact number on your dog's temporary ID and the lost dog flyer.

SEASONAL CONSIDERATIONS

Summer heat can be taxing on your dog, however, the dry heat of the West is more tolerable than the humidity of the South and East.

Dehydration and Heat Stroke

1. Hike in the early morning or late afternoon.
2. Carry at least 8 ounces of water per dog for each hour on the trail or 3 miles of hiking.
3. Rest in a shaded area during the intensity of the midday.
4. Take frequent rest stops and offer your dog water.
5. Let him take a plunge in a lake or lie belly down in a stream or mud puddle to cool.

Winter conditions will affect your dog's feet, her endurance, and her body warmth. Crusty snow can chafe and cut her pads, and walking in deep snow is very taxing and can put a shorthair dog at risk of hypothermia and frostbite.

Snow Safety

1. Carry booties for icy conditions and use them on dogs not accustomed to winter conditions. Take a couple extras as replacement for the ones lost in the snow. Keeping your dog on leash while he is in booties makes it easier to know when to adjust them or retrieve one's that drop off.
2. Consider a wool or polypropylene sweater for a shorthair dog.
3. Encourage your dog to walk behind you in your tracks. It is less strenuous.
4. Take a small sled or snow disk with an insulated foam pad so your dog can rest off the frozen ground.
5. Keep your outings short in winter, and carry snacks like liver or jerky treats and warm drinking water.

Spring, in some parts of the country, means heavy rain, mosquitoes, fleas, ticks, and a new crop of poison oak and ivy. Find out what you are in for so you can be prepared.

Fall announces hunting season in many parts of the backcountry. Check the hunting regulations and dates for the hiking area you have in mind. Most important, you and your dog should wear bright colors when hiking anywhere in the fall. Orange hunting vests are available for dogs, and colorful harnesses and bandannas are a good idea. When in doubt about hunting, keep your dog on a leash on forested trails.

COMMUNICATING WITH YOUR DOG

Your dog's two ways of communicating with you are through body language and vocal sounds. Listen to what he is trying to tell you by paying attention to his changes in demeanor on the trail. He is giving you important information about how he feels physically and his concerns about what awaits around the bend.

Body language: When everything is okay, your dog will have a light relaxed sway and an energetic bounce in his step. Ears suddenly forward and tail up or raised hackles (hair standing up on the back of his neck or base of the tail) indicate tension and alertness triggered by a smell, sound, or sight.

Vocal communication: If your dog appears uneasy, hyperactive, and alert and begins to bark, growl, or whine, she could be sensing a possible threat. The unusual smell, sound, or sight may not be visible to you, but respect her concern. Stop, listen, and look around. Pat your dog and speak to her reassuringly while keeping your wits about you. Make sure your dog is leashed and proceed cautiously until you identify the source of her concern, which can be as simple as another hiker around the bend or a rodent in the bushes.

Be sensitive: Tail down, stiff gait, and a lethargic pace may indicate a tightening of your dog's back or hip muscles from straining or bruising of soft tissue. Examine him carefully, checking his paws and between the toes for cuts or foreign bodies that could be causing him discomfort or pain. If he appears okay, stop, rest, and make sure he gets water. He may need a snack to boost his energy.

If your dog looks drained, demoralized, or sick; is injured; or you cannot explain his odd behavior, trust that something is wrong. Dogs in general have an almost misplaced desire to please even when in pain. Be considerate of your best friend's needs and limitations. Do not push him and jeopardize his well-being to meet your expectations and goals. On the trail you are a team and your teammate depends on you. Alter the route, and when in doubt cut the excursion short. In the unfortunate event that there is something serious going on with your dog, you may have to carry him out. You want to share safe positive experiences that will nurture his enthusiasm for hiking.

On the other hand, fatigue at the end of the day is normal. A mellow dog after a solid day's work and play on the trail is a good thing. After a meal and a good night's rest, your dog should emerge refreshed in the morning. If he's dragging, take it easy by hiking a shorter distance to your next campsite or making extra rest stops on the way to the car if this is the end of the trip.

PREVENTIVE CARE

Let your dog's pace determine the pace of the hike. Keep her on leash during the first 30 minutes of the hike. Off leash fresh out of the starting gate she may run around in a burst of energy and tucker herself out too soon because she has no way of knowing to pace herself if this is not a routine hike.

Stop frequently for water breaks and use the stops to examine her from head to tail. Remove the packs and check for chafing. Run your hands along her body feeling for foxtails and burrs before they become a problem. Check her feet for worn pads and foreign bodies lodged between the toes.

Nuisance Plants

Of all the plant nuisances, foxtails, found in the western U.S., can cause the most problems. At their worst in late summer and early fall, the arrow-like grasses are dry, sharp, and just waiting to burrow in some dog's fuzzy coat. The dry foxtail can be inhaled by a dog, lodge itself in the ear canal or between the toes, and camouflage itself in the dog's undercoat, puncturing the skin and causing infection. Foxtails have the potential of causing damage to vital organs.

Inspect your dog's ears and toes, and run your hands through his coat inspecting under the belly, legs, and tail. Brush his coat out after excursions where there were even hints of foxtails. Violent sneezing and snorting is an indication he may have inhaled a foxtail. Even if the sneezing or shaking decreases in intensity or frequency, the foxtail can still be tucked where it irritates only occasionally while it travels deeper and causes more serious damage. Contact a vet as soon as possible. Your dog may have to be anesthetized to remove the foxtail.

Poison Ivy and Poison Oak

These three-leaved low-growing plants (poison oak has shiny leaves) can cause topical irritations on hairless areas of your dog's body (you can apply cortisone cream to the affected area). Find out if there is poison ivy (usually in the Eastern states) or poison oak (mainly in the West) where you plan to

Poison Ivy   *Poison Oak*

hike and make sure you wash your hands with soap after handling your dog. The resin can rub off your dog onto you, your sleeping bag, car seat, and furniture at home. If you are very sensitive to these rashes, bathe your dog after the hike and sponge your arms and legs with a dilution of chlorine bleach before showering.

Other Poisonous Plants

Unfortunately, your dog may have the temptation to chew and taste hazardous plants. This includes plants found in your backyard, like rhubarb. However, in the wilderness, there are similar dangers—plants such as rhododendrons and Japanese yew may cause considerable sickness and discomfort for your pet. If you suspect poisoning, take note of what your dog ate and head back to the car. Once out of the woods, call your vet or an animal poison control center. See Appendix E for contact information.

FLEAS AND TICKS

Fleas are uncomfortable for your dog and carry tapeworm eggs, and ticks are one of nature's most painfully potent and tenacious creatures for their size. Some ticks cause uncomfortable red swollen irritation to the area of the skin where they attach or inflict temporary paralysis. Other types of ticks carry Rocky Mountain spotted fever and Lyme disease—reported to be the most common tick-carried disease in the United States.

Where Do Dogs Get Ticks?

Ticks thrive on wild hosts (deer are the most common) around lakes, streams, meadows, and some wooded areas. Ticks cling to the unsuspecting hiker or dog. On dogs they crawl out of the fur and attach to the skin around the neck, face, ears, stomach, or any soft fleshy cavity. They attach to their hosts by sticking their mouthparts into the skin to feed on the host's blood.

Removing a Tick

1. Try not to break off any mouthparts (remaining parts can cause infections), and avoid getting tick fluids on you through crushing or puncturing the tick.
2. Rotate the tick clockwise and counterclockwise with your fingertips to loosen its grip.
3. Applying petroleum jelly on the tick is sometimes successful in loosening its grip.
4. Grasp the tick as close to the skin as possible with blunt forceps, tweezers, or with your fingers in rubber gloves, tissue, or any barrier to shield your skin from possible tick fluids.
5. Remove the tick with a steady pull.
6. After removing the tick, disinfect the skin with alcohol and wash your hands with soap and water.

There is an abundance of chemical and natural flea and tick products on the market, including collars, dips, sprays, powders, pills, and oils. Some are effective on both fleas and ticks, remain effective on wet dogs, and require an easy once-a-month topical application. Consult your veterinarian about a safe and appropriate product.

MOSQUITOES

Avon's Skin-So-Soft is a less toxic and more pleasant smelling repellant, though it is not as effective as repellants containing deet. Mix 1 cap of the oil with 1 pint of water in a spray bottle. Spray your dog and run your hands through her coat from head to toe and tail to cover her with a light film of the mixture. Be careful to avoid her eyes and nostrils, but do not miss the outer ear areas.

WILDLIFE CONFLICTS

Most hikers with dogs come to the natural world "in peace" to retreat and absorb the beauty. Nevertheless, you are still an uninvited guest at best. Respect the animals whose home you are in and trespass lightly.

Protecting Wildlife

Leashes are mandatory in many outdoor recreation areas primarily to protect the wildlife that lives, breeds, migrates, or nests there. Even in areas where your dog is allowed off leash, do not let him chase wildlife or livestock for sport. It stresses and depletes the animal of survival energy and can cause a serious injury that leads to a cruel, agonizing death. Some dogs love to roll in fresh cow pies, another good reason to keep your dog leashed around cattle.

In the spring nesting birds are vulnerable to free-roaming dogs in meadows and low brush. Young deer can be separated from their mothers and fall prey to your dog's primal but inappropriate impulses.

Your companion is more likely to chase wildlife at the beginning of the hike, when he is fresh out of the starting gate. Keep him on leash for about 30 minutes while he walks off some of his excess energy and gets used to his surroundings.

If you have any doubts about your dog's behavior, keep him leashed.

Preventing Encounters

The potential for being injured or killed by a wild animal is extremely low compared with many other natural hazards. Information and preparation is the safest way for hikers with dogs to enjoy their time on the trail. When given the opportunity, most wild animals are more than happy to avoid humans; unfortunately, people often feed wild animals because they look cute and cuddly. Once a wild animal gets a taste of human food, it becomes habituated to human food and will not forget that humans are a source of food. Wild animals that have grown accustomed to human food and garbage can become brazen, posing a threat to human safety. In bears, these bad "man engendered" habits identify them as "problem" bears, which sadly leads to their eventual and inevitable destruction. If you love wild animals, respect them, admire them from a safe distance, and do not feed them. Remember, a fed bear is a dead bear.

Be informed about where you plan to hike and what lives there. Contact the region's fish and game, park, or forest headquarters. Keep your eyes open and learn to identify tracks, scat, and concealed kill sites. Keep your dog on a leash in questionable surroundings. Do not be shocked if your dog snacks on scat; it is a delicacy to some canines as is horse dung, known in some circles as trail muffins.

Bears and Bear Safety

There is no scientific evidence that dogs are bear bait. But a loose dog in bear country runs more of a chance of surprising a bear and antagonizing it with barking and other antics. Even if your dog gets lucky and runs back to you unharmed, your problems are just beginning if the bear follows. So use caution and think carefully about keeping your dog on leash in bear country.

Stay on the trail where there are fewer chances of surprising a bear snacking in a berry patch. Make your presence

BEAR FACTS
Bears can run, swim, and climb trees.
Bears have good vision, excellent hearing, and a superior sense of smell.
Bears are curious and attracted to food smells.
Bears can be out any time of day, but are most active in the coolness of dawn and dusk and after dark.
Bears and wild animals in general prefer anonymity. If they know you are out there, they will avoid your path.

known with noise that is distinctly manmade, like talking, singing, or humming a tune. The slight jingle of a metal ID tag against the metal rabies tag acts like a bell on your dog's collar or harness and can help notify bears of your presence. A small bell on the dog collar is a stronger statement in grizzly country.

When it comes to odor, in bear country the motto is "less is safer." Pack all food items (human and dog) and any odorous items in airtight zip-locked bags. Dispose of all items with food smells in airtight bags in bear-proof storage containers. Clean your dishes and pet bowls as quickly as possible so food smells do not float through the forest as a dinner invitation to the local bears. Some national forests and wilderness areas require that campers use plastic portable "bear resistant food canisters." These canisters (some collapsible) are available for sale and rent at sporting good stores and some ranger stations.

If you see a bear in the distance, stop, stay calm, and do not run. Keep your dog close to your side on leash. You should feel awe rather than panic. Walk a wide upwind detour so the animal can get your scent and make loud banging or clanging noises as you leave the area. If the bear is at closer range, the same principles apply while you keep your eye on the bear and back down the trail slowly if the terrain doesn't allow you to negotiate a detour.

Avoid sudden movements that could spook or provoke the bear. Be cool, slow, but deliberate as you make your retreat. (To learn more about hiking in bear country, refer to *Bear Aware*, by Bill Schneider [Falcon Publishing, 1996.])

Mountain Lions

There are fewer mountain lions than bears and the mountain lion population is concentrated in the western United States and Canada. As with bears, development and human intrusion are at the core of the encounter problems. Here are some tips to help you keep your pet safe from mountain lions:

- Keep your dog on leash on the trail.
- Keep her in the tent at night.
- Seeing does not mean attacking. If you come across a mountain lion, stay far enough away to give it the opportunity to avoid you.

MOUNTAIN LION FACTS
Mountain lions are elusive, and preying on humans is uncharacteristic.
Mountain lions are most active at dawn and dusk and they usually hunt at night.
They are solitary and secretive and require a vegetated habitat for camouflage while they stalk prey.
Their meal of choice is big game (deer, bighorn sheep, and elk). However, in the absence of game, they can make a meal of domestic livestock and small mammals.
They feed on what they kill. An unattended dog in camp is far more appetizing than his kibble.

Hiker looking big and intimidating

- Do not approach or provoke the lion.
- Walk away slowly and maintain eye contact. Running will stimulate the lion's predatory instinct to chase and hunt.
- Make yourself big by putting your arms above your head and waving them. Use your jacket or walking stick above your head to appear bigger. Do not bend down or make any motion that will make you look or sound like easy prey.
- Shout and make noise.
- If necessary, walking sticks can be weapons, as can rocks or anything you can get your hands on to fight back.

(For more information on hiking in mountain lion country, refer to *Mountain Lion Alert*, by Steven Torres [Falcon
Publishing 1997.])

Skunks

Skunks and porcupines are primarily nocturnal and will fend
off the curious with their juicy stench and barbed needles.
When your dog gets skunked, a potent smelly cloud of spray
burns his eyes and makes his mouth foam. The smell can
make you gag, and contact with the spray on your dog's coat
can give your skin a tingling, burning sensation. Apply
deskunking shampoo as soon as possible. Put on rubber
gloves and thoroughly wet your dog, apply the mixture, and
let stand for 15 minutes; rinse and repeat as needed.

Deskunking shampoo mix

1 quart hydrogen peroxide

1/4 cup baking soda

1 tablespoon dishwashing detergent

Porcupine Quills

A dog pierced by a mask of porcupine quills is a pitiful sight.
Some hikers carry vinegar to soften the quills and make them
easier to remove. Extract quills by grasping them at the base
of the point of penetration with pliers. The discomfort and
pain of having barbed needles pulled out of their faces can
make dogs unpredictable, and removing quills can be dangerous for inexperienced hands. Take your dog to a vet as
quickly as possible.

Snakes and Spiders

Most dogs have an instinctive aversion to lizards and snakes. Snakebites are usually a result of stepping on the snake unknowingly rather than conscious provocation. Most snakebites occur on the nose or front legs and can be lethal to a small or young dog. If taken to the vet quickly larger adult dogs will survive the bite. Black widow venom can be more lethal than snake venom. Seek veterinary attention. For puncture wounds, keep your dog calm (activity stimulates the absorption of venom), rinse the area with water, and transport your dog to the nearest vet.

Bees, wasps, hornets, and yellow jackets

A leash is the best preventive measure to protect your dog from her own curiosity. Nests can be in trees or on the ground. Bee stings and spider bites may cause itching, swelling, and hives. If the stinger is still present, scrape it off with your nail or tweezers at the base away from the point of entry (pressing the stinger or trying to pick it from the top can release more toxins). Apply a cold compress to the area and spray it with a topical analgesic like Benadryl spray to relieve the itch and pain. As a precaution carry an over-the-counter antihistamine (such as Benadryl) and ask your vet about the appropriate dosage before you leave, in case your dog has an extreme allergic reaction with excessive swelling.

DOG AID ON THE TRAIL

Care and caution are the first steps on the way to a good

time and memorable experience with your dog. Planning, a commonsense approach, and a leash will help prevent most mishaps on the trail.

Keep Your Dog on Leash When . . .

- Hiking in territory known for its higher concentration of specific hazards (bears, mountain lions, snakes, skunks)
- Crossing fast-moving streams
- Negotiating narrow mountainside trails
- Hiking in wind and snow (dogs can become disoriented and lose their way).

Basic First-Aid Treatment

Bleeding from cuts or wounds:

1. Remove any obvious foreign object
2. Rinse the area with warm water or 3% hydrogen peroxide
3. Cover the wound with a clean gauze or cloth and apply firm, direct pressure over the wound for at about 10 minutes to allow clotting and bleeding to stop
4. Place a nonstick pad or gauze over the wound and bandage with gauze wraps (the stretchy, clingy type). For a paw wound, cover the bandaging with a bootie. (An old sock with duct tape on the bottom is a good bootie substitute. Use adhesive tape around the sock to prevent it from slipping off.)
5. Get your pet to the veterinarian.

Heatstroke (the dog's body temperature is rising rapidly above 104 degrees F and panting is ineffective to regulate temperature): Get your dog out of the sun and begin reducing body temperature (no lower than 103 degrees F) by applying water-soaked towels on her head (to cool the brain), chest, abdomen, and feet. Let her stand in a pond, lake, or stream while you gently pour water on her. Avoid icy water—it can chill her. Swabbing the footpads with alcohol will help.

Hypothermia (the body temperature drops below 95 degrees F because of overexposure to cold weather): Take the dog indoors or in to a sheltered area where you can make a fire. Wrap him in a blanket, towel, sleeping bag, your clothing, or whatever you have available. Wrap warm towels or place warm water bottles next to him and hold him close to you for body heat.

Frostbite (the freezing of a body part exposed to extreme cold; tips of the ears and pads are the most vulnerable): Remove your dog from the cold. Apply warm compresses to the affected area without friction or pressure.

Sore muscles (aches and tightness in the limbs and hip area from excessive activity): Rest your dog apply cold water to compress tight muscle areas to reduce inflammation.

Cardiopulmonary resuscitation (CPR): Check with your vet or local humane society for pet CPR classes.

10

Trail Etiquette

Trail etiquette boils down to good dog manners and reliability. Even in areas where a leash is not mandatory, control is. Dogs can be shot for harassing livestock and wildlife. Trail etiquette is especially important for maintaining good relations between those with and without dogs.

At one time or another, your dog may be a partner in a dominance dance with another dog. It is more frequent between males, especially intact males that reek of testosterone. Dogs well versed in pack hierarchy know to stay out of an alpha dog's face or to assume the subordinate body language that stops the music.

MINIMIZE DOG–DOG CONFLICTS

Neuter your male dog before 1 one year of age or as soon as both testicles drop. Overt dominance may not appear until he is two years of age. Neutering reduces macho and roaming instincts. Be aware that testosterone levels take several months to decrease after neutering.

Spay your female. Breeding females can be instinctively more competitive around other females. A female in season should never be on the trail. She will create havoc and her mating instincts will override her flawless obedience record of accomplishment for sure.

A leashed dog can be overly protective. *Avoid stress* by making a detour around other hikers with dogs, or stepping off the trail with your dog at a sit while the other hiker and dog walk by.

Do not panic at the hint of raised hackles and loud talk. It is just posturing. If your dog is off leash, keep walking away from the other dog while encouraging your dog to come in your most enthusiastic voice and with the promise of a biscuit. If she complies, reward her with a "good dog" and the promised biscuit for positive reinforcement. Walking back toward the dogs screaming and interfering before they resolve their conflict can stoke the fires of a more serious brawl. If the squabble escalates into a dogfight, make sure you cover your arms and hands before trying to break it up. Pull the dogs by the tail, lift their hind legs off the ground, or throw water on them to distract them. As a last resort, you may have to throw sand or dirt in the eyes of the one with the grip to pry her away. One hiker who uses a cane as a hiking stick reports having broken up a dogfight or two by slipping the crook of his cane under the dog collar or harness to drag the thug away.

Do not give treats to other hikers' dogs. Competition for food and protection of territory are the root of most dog fights.

LOW IMPACT DOG HIKING

As our exploding urban populations rush to retreat in the backcountry, our fragile and diminishing ecosystems are at greater risk of collapsing under the weight of our hiking boots. More people competing for the use of limited recreation areas leave dog owners vulnerable to criticism.

- Pack out everything you pack in.
- Do not leave dog scat on the trail. Bury it away from the trail and surface water. Or, better yet, carry plastic bags for removal. Obey all regulations regarding pet litter.
- Hike only where dogs are permitted and abide by the regulations posted.
- Stay on the trail and in designated campsites in heavily used or developed areas.
- Step lightly in more remote pristine areas.
- Do not let your dog chase wildlife.
- Do not let your dog charge other dogs or hikers, regardless of his harmless exuberance and friendly intentions. A leash is a great pacifier around people who may not be comfortable with dogs.
- Dogs can spook horses and pack stock, putting riders in danger. Step off the trail and wait with your dog at a sit position until the traffic has passed. Always leash your dog when passing other hikers, cyclists, horseback riders, or anyone with whom you are sharing the trail.
- Do not let your dog bark at hikers, pack animals, wildlife, or at the moon. It is intrusive to those who choose hiking as an escape to quiet and serenity.

*On the trail with your dog, yield to other
hikers and wildlife*

Some hikers have strong opinions about why dogs should not be allowed in the backcountry. Avoid debating the issue of "hiking with dogs" with other hikers. Every hiker with a dog is an ambassador for all dog owners. Be courteous and use this opportunity to influence their opinion by keeping your dog on his best backcountry behavior.

Hiking on Public Lands

The United States has an extensive network of public lands available for recreation. They are divided in categories by use and administered by different governmental agencies from the regional to federal level. Following are general descriptions and distinctions within our public land system and examples of various dog policies.

The National Park Service oversees several hundred parks, historic sites, monuments, and recreation areas. The Park Service's first priority is conservation. Dogs are required to be on leash or physically restrained at all times; they may be permitted in the paved developed outdoor areas (frontcountry) but almost never on the hiking trails (backcountry). Some of the exceptions to the rule include Devil's Tower National Monument, Wyoming; Devil's Postpile National Monument, California; Shenandoah National Park, Virginia; Acadia National Park, Maine; Mount Rushmore National Memorial, South Dakota; and Chiricahua National Monument, Arizona.

National recreation areas provide a playground for a broad range of outdoor activities with an emphasis on water sports. Many allow dogs on leash. *National lakeshores, rivers,* and *seashores* are three other categories within the national park system with varying dog policies. *Grasslands* cover one-quarter of the earth's surface. In the United States, the National Grasslands agency is a recent project created to restore and preserve one of our most productive and abused ecosystems. National grasslands permit wandering off trail, picking grasses and flowers, and collecting rocks. Dogs on leash or under voice control are welcome.

The Bureau of Land Management is a multiple-use resource agency and leans toward dog-friendly regulations. The BLM's 270 million acres were once described as "the lands nobody wanted," but outdoor enthusiasts recognize the recreational value of the West's rugged BLM lands.

National forests were conceived 100 years ago to combine use and conservation. The nearly 200 national forests are scattered from coast to coast and stretch from Alaska to Puerto Rico, providing the largest number of dog-compatible hiking trails. Dog regulations vary from leash to voice control.

State parks are not among the most dog-friendly hiking grounds, but some, like Custer State Park in South Dakota and Smith Rock State Park in Oregon, allow leashed dogs on trails.

Preserves and reserves can be found in both the public and private land banks. The primary concern here is preservation and conservation. In some preserves dog restrictions are seasonal, based on wildlife breeding and nesting cycles.

Others, like Point Lobos State Reserve in Carmel, California, prohibit dogs from even entering the park in your vehicle. The state of massachusetts has an extensive network of land conservation agencies, with several wildland preserves on such islands as Martha's Vineyard and Nantucket.

County and regional parks: Some are expansive parks and provide excellent day hiking. Use regulations vary with each park from "no dogs allowed" to dogs under voice control. Grazing cattle is a common determining factor in dog policy.

North of the border: Many Canadian provincial and national parks allow leashed dogs on trails.

There is no better playground than the wilds of our public lands, and no better playmate than your dog. Plan, prepare, and safely share your best moments on the trail with your dog. Remember to pack the snacks, water, leash, and good sense and trail manners. Take good care of your hiking companion and he or she will take care of you.

Happy Trails!

Checklists

DAY HIKE CHECKLIST

☐ Apply flea and tick treatment prior to hike.

☐ Bug repellent in sealed plastic bag.

☐ Health and vaccination certificate.

☐ Collar and bandanna or colorful harness with permanent and temporary ID tag and rabies tag.

☐ Leather leash or expandable leash.

☐ Plastic water containers full of water: 32-ounce bottle for half-day hike (under 4 hours) and 2-quart bottle for longer hikes.

☐ Plan to carry 8 ounces of water per dog per hour or 3 miles of hiking, in addition to water for you.

☐ Water purifier for full-day hikes.

☐ Snacks for you and your pet.

☐ Collapsible dish or zip-locked bag.

☐ Plastic bags for cleaning up after your dog.

☐ Sunscreen for tips of ears and nose.

☐ Booties for pooch and comfortable, sturdy, and waterproof boots for you.

☐ Extra clothing (sweater or coat for thin-coated dog, sweater, waterproof windbreaker, windpants, and hat with brim for you).

- [ ] Daypack
- [ ] Whistle.
- [ ] Plastic trowel and toilet paper.
- [ ] Extra large, heavy-duty plastic garbage bags (good to sit on and make a handy poncho in the rain).
- [ ] Flyers for a lost dog.
- [ ] Topographic map.
- [ ] Pencil and paper.
- [ ] Pocketknife (Swiss Army knife that includes additional tools: fork, scissors, pliers, file).
- [ ] Flashlight and extra batteries.
- [ ] Matches or cigarette lighter and emergency fire starter.
- [ ] Compass.
- [ ] First-aid kit.
- [ ] Telephone number and address of closest veterinarian.

BACKPACKING CHECKLIST

All items on day hike checklist plus the following:

- [ ] Extra leash or rope.
- [ ] Dog packs for pooch and backpack with internal frame for you.
- [ ] Doggie bedroll (foam sleeping pad).
- [ ] Dog's favorite chew toy.
- [ ] Dog food (number of days on the trail times three meals a day).
- [ ] Additional water in a 2-quart bottle.
- [ ] Water purifier.
- [ ] Dog snacks (enough for six rest stops per hiking day).

- ☐ Collapsible food and water dish (zip-locked bags).
- ☐ Tie-out rope in camp (expandable leash can be extra leash and tie-out rope).
- ☐ Human clothing (long pants; rain jacket and pants; gloves; knit hat; extra socks, polypropelene and fleece).
- ☐ Camp stove, pots, cup, bowl, and eating utensils.
- ☐ Fuel and fuel bottle.
- ☐ Pans and eating utensils.
- ☐ Nylon cord.
- ☐ Iodine tablets (back-up water purification).
- ☐ Human food (around 1 pound per person per day).
- ☐ Human snacks.
- ☐ Human sleeping bag and pad.
- ☐ Tent with rain fly (large enough for both you and your dog to sleep inside).
- ☐ Additional garbage bags.
- ☐ Permit (if required).
- ☐ Pepper spray (if hiking in bear country).

FIRST-AID KIT

- ☐ First-aid book (see Appendix D for some suggestions).
- ☐ Muzzle—the most loving dogs can snap and bite when in pain. Muzzles come in different styles and sizes to fit all dog nose shapes.
- ☐ Ascriptin (buffered aspirin)—older dogs in particular may be stiff and sore at the end of a hike or a backpacking excursion. Consult your vet on the appropriate dosage for your dog's size.

- Scissors (rounded tips) to trim hair around a wound.
- Hydrogen peroxide (3 percent) to disinfect surface abrasions and wounds.
- Antiseptic ointment.
- Gauze pads and gauze.
- Clingy and elastic bandages.
- Sock or bootie to protect a wounded foot.
- Duct tape to wrap around a sock used as a bootie.
- Tweezers to remove ticks, needles, or foreign objects in a wound.
- Petroleum jelly to cover a tick.
- Pliers for porcupine quills.
- Moleskin/blister kit.
- Styptic powder for bleeding.
- Rectal thermometer.
- Hydrocortisone spray to relieve plant rashes and stings.
- Space blanket.
- Your veterinarian's telephone number and telephone number of the veterinary clinic closest to the trailhead.
- Skunk juice recipe (keep 1 quart of the mixture in your car, ready to use).

Trail Treat Recipe

PHIL'S LIVER AND ONION CHEWS

2-1/2 cups rye flour or soybean flour

1/2 cup powdered milk

1/2 teaspoon onion powder

6 tablespoons margarine

1 egg well beaten

4 tablespoons liver powder

1/2 cup water

Cooking Instructions: To make liver powder, microwave 1/4 pound of chopped liver for 5 minutes or until dry enough to crumble into powder. Preheat oven to 350 degrees F. Combine flour, dry milk, and onion powder. Add margarine to the mixture. Add 1 beaten egg and 4 tablespoons liver powder. Add 1/2 cup cold water and roll mixture into a ball. Roll dough 1/2 inch thick onto a lightly greased cookie sheet. Cut with a dog biscuit cutter or cookie cutter of your choice. Gather remaining dough scraps into a ball, roll out, and cut. Bake for 25 to 30 minutes at 350 degrees F.

Sources of Dog Hiking Gear and Accessories

Mail-order catalogs:

Dog's Life Inc.
P.O. Box 251
Yachats, OR 97498
541-547-3464
Info@dogs-life.com

In the Company of Dogs
P.O. Box 1075
Beverly, MA 01915-0775
800-924-5050

R. C. Steele
P.O. Box 910
Brockport, NY 14420-0910
800-872-3773

Wolf Packs
Ashland, OR 97520-9408
541-482-7669
www.wolfpacks.com

Suggested Reading

A Guide to Backpacking with Your Dog
   by Charlene G. Labelle
   Alpine Publications

The Whole Dog Catalog
   by John Avalon
   Three Rivers Press

Dogs on the Web
   by Audrey Pavia and Betsy Sikora Siino
   MIS Press

The Wolf Within
   by David Alderton
   Howell Book House

Can You Turn a Wolf into a Dog
   by Pat Tucker and Bruce Weide
   (Send $2.00 to Wild Sentry/Hybrid Booklet, P.O. Box
   172, Hamilton, MT 59840)

Dog Fancy Magazine
   Fancy Publications, P.O. Box 6050
   Mission Viejo, CA 92690
   (714) 855-8822

Resources

The American Animal Hospital Association offers veterinarian referrals. 800-252-2242. Tape the phone number inside your first-aid kit.

American Automobile Association. Membership gives you access to tour books and camp books (free of charge) for every state and province. Each tour book includes a list and map of national, state, and other recreational areas, including a chart indicating which have hiking trails and allow pets on leash. 1-800-JOIN-AAA; www.csaa.com.

The American Kennel Club in Raleigh, North Carolina, offers breeder referrals and information about the Canine Good Citizen training program in your community. 919-233-9767.

ASPCA-National Animal Poison Control Center, www.napcc.aspca.org. 800-548-2423/900-680-0000. (Free for states with subsidized federal funding, but $30/per consultation otherwise.)

ATC (Appalachian Trail Conference). 304-535-6331; atconf.org.

Dog Hikers of Georgia. 24-hour Dog Hiker Hotline 770-992-2362.

About the Author

Linda Mullally is a freelance writer who divides her time at home between Carmel Valley and Mammoth, California. She was the first travel columnist for Dog Fancy, sharing information about dog-friendly getaways domestically and abroad while giving readers safety and responsible dog ownership tips. Dogs and hiking have always been a part of her life. She shares her adventures with her husband, David, an outdoor photographer, and their two dogs, Lobo and Shiloh. *Hiking with Dogs* is her first book.